Wings
Wheels

"Hiya, I'm Zeek."

"Hi, I'm Finn."

Calling all aliens!

Are you planning a holiday to planet Earth?

'Wings and Wheels'
Published by MAVERICK ARTS PUBLISHING LTD
Studio 11, City Business Centre, 6 Brighton Road,
Horsham, West Sussex, RH13 5BB, +44 (0)1403 256941
© Maverick Arts Publishing Limited November 2019

A CIP catalogue record for this book is available at the British Library.

ISBN 978-1-84886-633-1

Maverick publishing
www.maverickbooks.co.uk

Credits:
Finn & Zeek illustrations by Jake McDonald, Bright Illustration Agency
Cover: Jake McDonald/Bright, Art Konovalov/Shutterstock.com
Inside: **Unsplash.com:** Tomas Anton Escobar (6), Jordan Sanchez (8), Hitesh Choudhary (10), Connor Williams (10), Miles Farnsworth (11), Elena Kuchko (11), Dakota Corbin (12), Francisco Requena (13), Max Böhme (14), Jonathan Chng (16), chuttersnap (17), Corry (17 & 28), Brigitta Schneiter (19), Fernando Jorge (20), Vidar Nordli-Mathisen (21), Peter Fleming (22), Christian Wiediger (23), Joonyeop Baek (24), James Homans (27). **Shutterstock.com:** Art Konovalov (10), iunewind (21), Electric Egg (25), bonandbon (25).

This book is rated as: Orange Band (Guided Reading)
This story is decodable at Letters and Sounds Phase 5.

Wings and Wheels

Contents

Introduction	4
Wings	8
Planes	8
Wheels	10
Cars	10
Bikes	12
Horses	14
Public Transport	16
Buses	16
Trains	17
Trams	18
Water	20
Ships	20
Boats	22
Other Ways to Go	24
Quiz	28
Index/Glossary	30

INCOMING MESSAGE

Dear Finn and Zeek,

We want to go to Earth for a holiday. But how will we get around, once we get there?

Can you show us how people travel on Earth?

From Torro and Rush
(Planet Vaycay)

Introduction

Earth is very big, with lots of land and lots of sea! There are many ways to get around.

Hurry up, Finn. I want to travel fast!

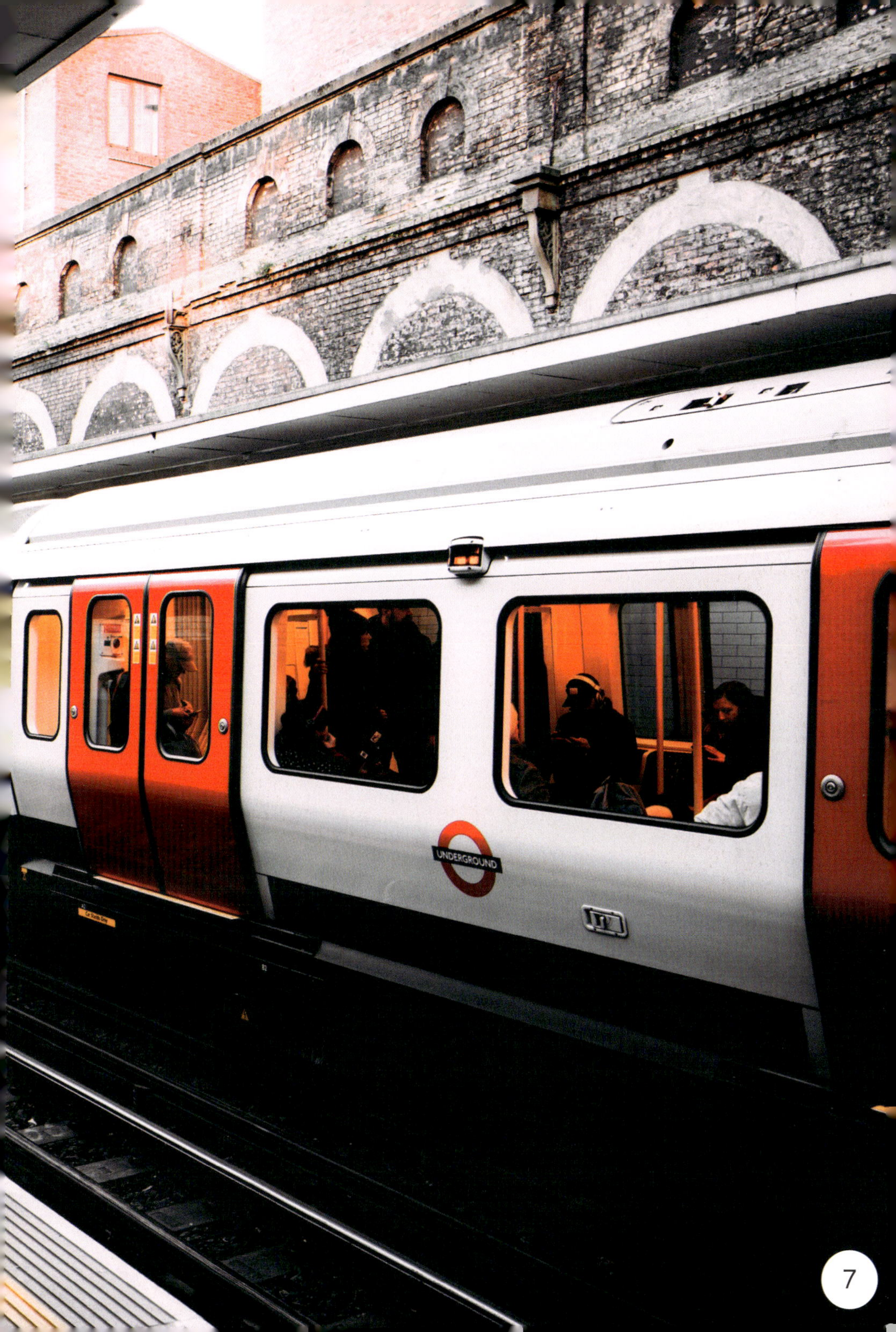
UNDERGROUND

Wings Planes

If you want to travel fast, a plane is a great choice! It flies high above the clouds and can go as fast as 600 miles per hour! Planes have large wings to help them fly.

Planes come in lots of different sizes. You can have lots of people on one plane, or just one!

It's a shame people don't have proper spaceships like us yet!

Wheels   Cars

Cars are very popular. Most people use cars to travel between towns and cities.

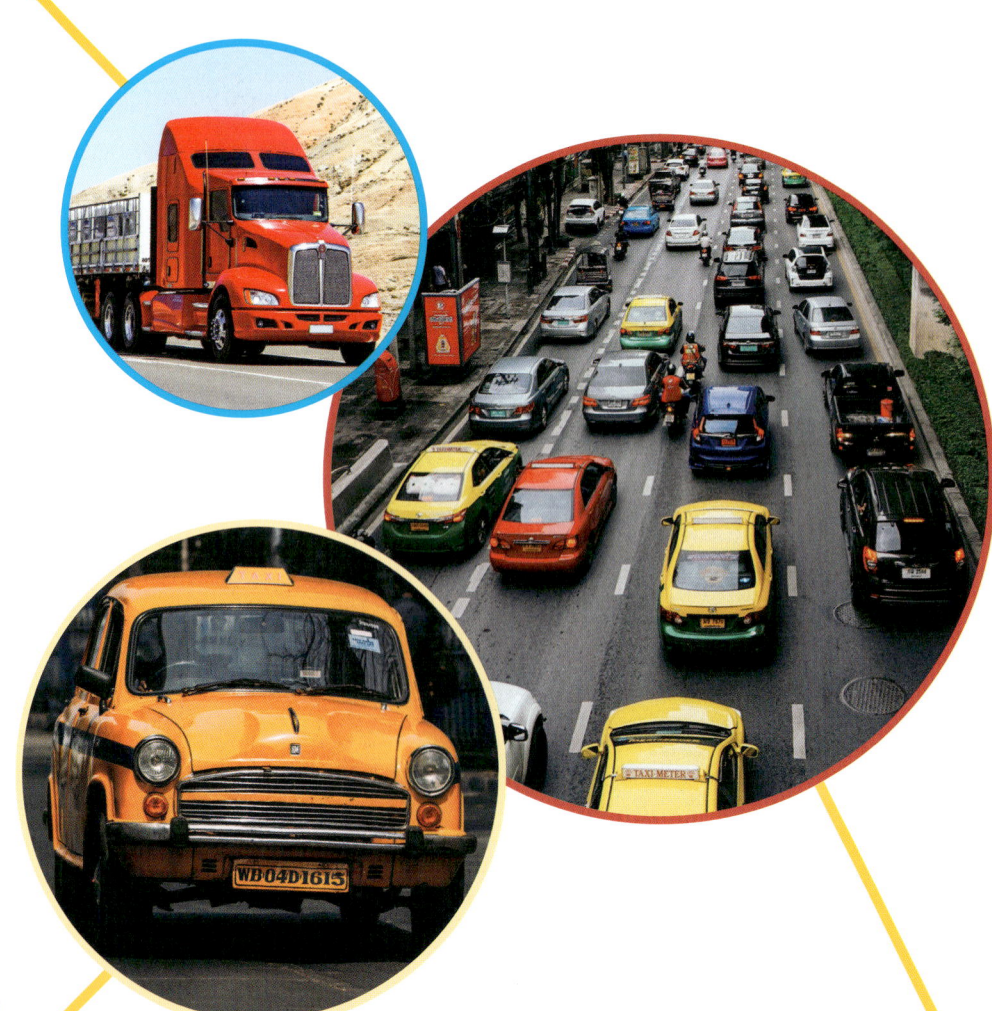

Cars usually have four wheels and are powered by **fuel**. The roads that cars drive on have speed limits.

That one looks like our spaceship!

Wheels Bikes

When you ride a bike, your legs do all the work! Your feet push the pedals, which turn the chain. The chain turns the wheels.

Motorbikes are like bikes, but need fuel to make them go. Most motorbikes can travel as fast as cars.

You should always wear a helmet when riding a bike!

Wheels | Horses

Animals can also help!

Before cars were invented, people often travelled by horse. Horses pulled carts with wheels, like this one.

That's why there's a unit of power called '**horsepower**'!

Public Transport — Buses

Buses can carry lots of people! The more people travel on buses, the fewer cars will be on the road. This helps to prevent **global warming**.

Trains

Trains are the fastest method of land travel. They are powered by electricity and run along tracks.

The first form of train was a steam train. These were powered by coal and let out a lot of smoke!

Public Transport — Trams

Trams are a mix between buses and trains. They run along tracks, but the tracks are on the same roads as cars. Trams are powered by electricity, like trains. But for trams, the power comes from a line above them.

Overhead Line

19

Water   Ships

Boats are a slower method of travel. Humans use cruise ships to travel overseas. These huge ships can hold up over 6,000 people.

Some ships are as high as a 16-storey building!

Cargo ships are like cruise ships, but for things instead of people! Some cargo ships can carry up to 564 metric tonnes of stuff. That's the same weight as 3.8 million apples!

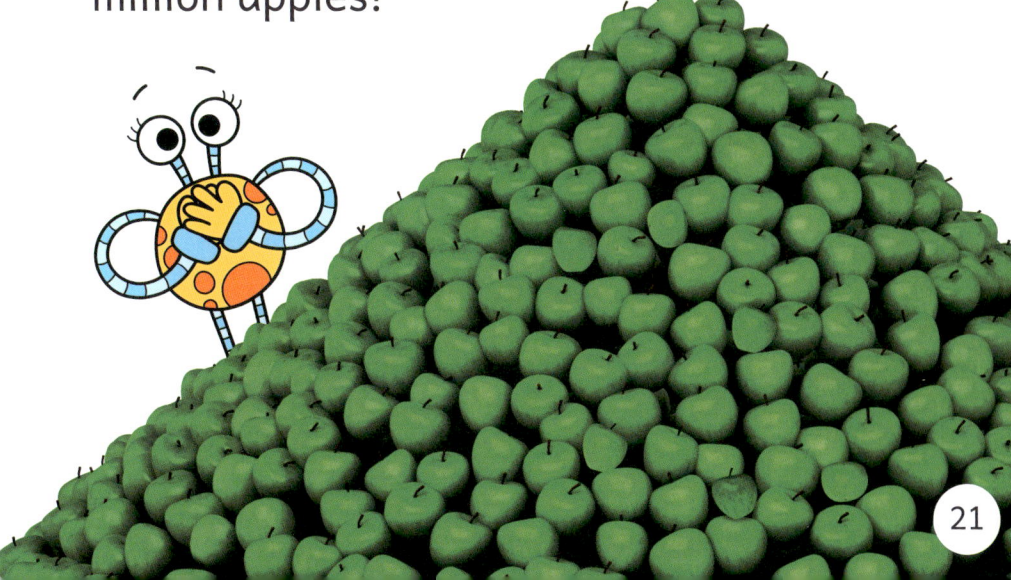

Water   Boats

Narrowboats like this one are used on canals. They are long and thin!

Two hundred years ago, narrowboats were pulled along by horses. The boats were used to carry heavy things like coal.

Sailing boats are powered by the wind.

These are used for fun, travel or fishing.

Some humans live on boats.

Other Ways to Go

Hot Air Balloons

Hot air balloons are a slow way to travel through the air. They were invented long before planes. A huge balloon is filled with hot air, and a **burner** heats the air to make the balloon go higher.

The tracks are up here!

Suspension Railway

In Wuppertal, Germany, there's a railway that's upside-down! The train hangs down from the track, high above the street.

MESSAGE SENT

Dear Torro and Rush,

As you can see, there are lots of different ways to get around Earth.

If you're looking for speed, planes are the best. But if you want to enjoy your surroundings, then we suggest the narrowboat!

From,
Finn and Zeek x

Some narrowboats are very pretty too!

Quiz

1. What helps planes fly?
a) Wheels
b) Small wings
c) Large wings

2. How many wheels does a car usually have?
a) 10
b) 4
c) 1

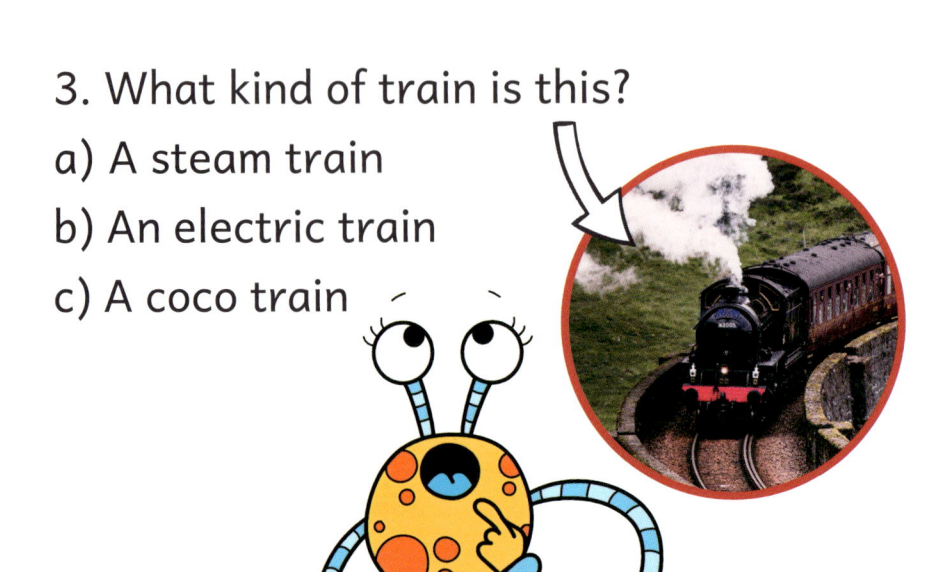

3. What kind of train is this?
a) A steam train
b) An electric train
c) A coco train

4. How much weight can a cargo ship hold?
a) 64 kilograms
b) 564 tonnes
c) 56 grams

5. When were narrowboats pulled by horses?
a) About 200 years ago
b) Over 2000 years ago
c) Only 2 years ago

6. Where might you find an upside-down railway?
a) Australia
b) England
c) Germany

Index/Glossary

Burner pg 24
The engine of a hot air balloon. It is what creates the hot air so that the balloon can rise.

Cargo pg 21
Items that are carried onboard a large transport such as a ship, train, truck, plane, etc.

Fuel pg 11, 13
Something that can be burned/used to make heat or power. There are many types of fuel, such as:
- Petrol
- Electricity
- Diesel

Quiz Answers:

1. c, 2. b, 3. a, 4. b, 5. a, 6. c

Global warming pg 16
The rising temperature of the Earth.

Horsepower pg 15
A unit of power that was made to compare the power of a horse with the power of a steam engine.

Book Bands for Guided Reading

The Institute of Education book banding system is a scale of colours that reflects the various levels of reading difficulty. The bands are assigned by taking into account the content, the language style, the layout and phonics. Word, phrase and sentence level work is also taken into consideration.

Maverick Early Readers are a bright, attractive range of books covering the pink to white bands. All of these books have been book banded for guided reading to the industry standard and edited by a leading educational consultant.

Pink
Red
Yellow
Blue
Green
Orange
Turquoise
Purple
Gold
White

Fiction

Non-fiction

To view the whole Maverick Readers scheme, visit our website at www.maverickearlyreaders.com

Or scan the QR code above to view our scheme instantly!